# THE AFTERNOON BEFORE THE DAY
# BEFORE THE NIGHT BEFORE
# CHRISTMAS

Nina hadn't intended on entering into the hidden space in the Lost Bookshop. The room that held the wonderful publications that blended the children away to unimaginable adventure. She thought she was meeting her pals and also switching Christmas presents. Things don't constantly go to strategy.

That specific day was the last Friday of school in December as well as points will go as far not-to-plan as it was possible to go.

Generally the home window of the store had plenty of unknown publications that held no passion to the kids. This year, nevertheless, Nina's Uncle Bill remained in the window putting the finishing touches to the tree. This was especially unexpected to Nina who constantly asked as well as asked as well as always got the very same 'no' in reply but this year ...

" Please can we have a tree in the home window Uncle Bill? Pleeeeeeease?" she had actually asked.

" Yes, pleeeeeeease," Nina's good friends Ivy as well as Oswald had actually chorused.

" Not bloomin' likely," Uncle Bill had responded firmly. "Don't want yearn needles and dirt as well as mess anywhere."

And after that a voice had actually drifted from one more space inside the store.

" Billy," claimed the voice. It was a voice they all recognised due to the fact that it was the voice of Nina's Aunty Ann. "Let's have a Christmas tree in the shop this year."

Therefore, amidst much huffing and also puffing and also muttering under his breath, Uncle Bill hadn't just headed out and purchased a tree. Instead, he had actually built a tree from eco-friendly hardback publications.

" But what if someone wishes to get among the books at the bottom of the pile?" Oswald had asked not long after it was ended up.

" Then that a person can get bound," responded Uncle Bill.

This wasn't a substantial surprise to Nina. She covertly thought her Uncle Bill ran the bookshop to save a collection that had long since outgrown his residence. Marketing books to clients was low on his list of concerns.

Previously in the month Nina had actually mosted likely to a great deal of difficulty to pick the excellent presents for Ivy and Oswald. Once the tree was finished she took the neatly-wrapped presents to it. Considering that Uncle Bill had actually built the tree from publications, she could not put them underneath. Instead, Nina placed them just in front of the tree, near to the home window to attempt to make Uncle Bill's decors look even better.

The last day of school meant that the 3 friends went out early. They had set up to meet up as well as exchange presents before the Christmas holidays started. Nina's ideal buddy Ivy arrived at Uncle Bill's office, deep in the bowels of the Lost Bookshop. She carefully took today for Oswald as well as Nina out of her bag as well as put them on Uncle Bill's workdesk. There was an open fire at the opposite of the office and Ivy strayed over and also made herself comfortable in front of it.

" Hey Ivy," said Oswald, going through the door. Prior to they had actually uncovered the hidden area the ladies had just recognized Oswald as, 'that kid who spends time the shop', yet after their very first enchanting adventure together, the three had come to be firm buddies. Oswald pushed his small, rounded glasses back onto the bridge of his nose after that thoroughly put the here and now he had actually caused the desk beside Ivy's prior to joining her in front of the fire.

Nina poked her head around the door.

" Hey you two," she claimed. "I'm just going to obtain your presents. Aid yourself to hot chocolate, I will not be long."

" Hot chocolate!" Ivy dashed out of Uncle Bill's office leaving a trail of blond hair in her wake.

Nina made her method to the window to order the pressies however to her scary, she discovered there had been a leak. The Lost Bookshop was old. Truly old. No-one recognized exactly how old other than, maybe for Uncle Bill as well as if he understood he had not been telling. The trouble with actually old buildings is that they sometimes don't hold with each other quite along with not-so-old structures. Nina appreciated see a big moist patch right above the area she had placed today. There was a steady drip-drip of water putting onto the presents she had purchased for her buddies.

She discharged a frustrated groan and also attempted to pick up Oswald's. The covering paper had been saturated to the factor where her fingers simply passed

right with it. Today inside was completely destroyed. She eyed her watch, it was far too late to head to one more store as well as change them. And afterwards Nina had an idea ...

Around her neck was a locket and also on that necklace was a trick - the trick to the concealed room. Before she had actually even considered it she located herself picking up her bag and sliding her arms into her layer. She opened the door to the concealed area, closing it silently behind her. Nina took a deep breath of the messy air of the completely rounded area. The normal smell of old publications existed however there was something behind-the-scenes. Heavy steam? Burning coal perhaps? She had actually never ever been on an experience without Ivy and also Oswald before yet she had actually snuck into the covert room as well as she kept in mind among the books. There was a market mentioned on the back cover. And also markets marketed presents. And she needed two presents today.

The shelves stretched from flooring to ceiling and Nina ran her fingers along the backs of the books till she discovered the one she was searching for, the one that in some way seemed to be phoning call to her.

She took a deep breath and afterwards checked in her pouch. There were a couple of points in there she might require, a torch, a headscarf, some earmuffs. She responded to herself then closed the bag and also looked at the cover of the book for a moment. After that, butterflies dancing in her belly, she opened the cover. Dirt started to swirl around the room, picking up speed, grabbing extra dirt and rotating and also rotating. The book flew from her hold as well as up around her head, circling method up towards the skylight, before eluding and diving in the direction of her. Nina squinted her eyes as the dirt swirled quicker and much faster till, with a thunderous bang, everything quit spinning and everything went dark.

# Chapter 2

## IN THE DARK AND OUT THE DOOR


Nina opened her eyes as well as wasn't surprised to find that she could not see anything at all. That sometimes taken place. She inhaled deeply through her nose as well as can smell old wood as well as natural leather. And after that the whole room moved from entrusted to appropriate and also she fell on her bottom.

" Ow!" she shouted as well as, producing her arms to stable herself, she was instantly able to feel a familiar rhythm.

She was on a train.

" Excellent," she said. "Just where I intended to be. And currently I'm speaking to myself. Hope there's nobody else in here or they'll believe I'm entirely cuckoo."

She awaited a moment. Listening in the darkness. Nobody responded so she very carefully got to her feet as well as extended out her arms till she can really feel a wood-panelled wall surface. When she had located that, she felt her means around the little space until she located the deal with of a door.

Great, she assumed as well as drew at the take care of. The door glided open and light and also sound spilled into the room.

Currently, you probably have 1 or 2 inquiries at this moment in our story so enable me to distract you for a minute and also attend to the most interesting of them. If this is your first see to the Lost Bookshop then perhaps you do not find out about the covert space. If that was the situation after that just how wrong you were, possibly you simply believed this was a story regarding a bookshop ....

The hidden room had not always been hidden, obviously, yet not long ago Uncle Bill had actually uncovered the door to it behind some shelfs. In some stores this might have been a surprise, but not in the Lost Bookshop. The place was a puzzle of spaces, hallways, shelves, cubbyholes, upstairs, downstairs as well as publications. Numerous books.

But the lure of a secured door and also possible adventure had enticed the 3 friends in. They had - fairly by accident - uncovered that there was magic in the web pages hereabouts.

Ever since Nina, Ivy and also Oswald had actually been on such journeys, the likes of which most normal youngsters would just dream around. Occasionally the adventures mored than swiftly, often they would certainly be shed in the tale for days or perhaps weeks. In spite of that, when they returned home, practically no time in all appeared to have actually passed.

It was this last fact that Nina was relying upon in her pursuit for presents. She knew that she might take her time inside this magic book since when she came back, Ivy and Oswald probably wouldn't also discover she had actually been gone.

Or that's what she hoped.

Anyhow, sufficient of my interruptions. I'm sure you are wondering where exactly Nina was and what got on the opposite side of that open door?

Excellent, I'm thankful.

Thankfully, Nina saw specifically what she hoped she would see, a corridor which stretched left and also right. It was full of people; males, women, children, ladies, all worn strange but brightly coloured foreign clothing. There was babbling and screaming in all kinds of languages as well as all type of individuals chuckling, saying as well as haggling. Somewhere she made sure she can make out the sound of a man's deep, deep voice vocal singing a soulful as well as unfortunate track.

As soon as she stepped into the corridor she knew she had picked exactly the ideal publication to obtain a present from. You see, Nina hadn't simply chosen the magical market publication by coincidence. Really little appeared to occur by chance in the Lost Bookshop. As a matter of fact she had been outlined the marketplace by her Aunty Ann. Someday, a couple of months ago, Aunty Ann had been waxing lyrical about a publication she assumed Nina must review. A publication that featured a magical area called The Clockwork Bazaar. Of course, her Aunty Ann didn't know that it was an actual area that you might actually go to. Or possibly she did ...

The Clockwork Bazaar was a market and also it was on a train. The tale, as Aunty Ann had actually defined it, included an antique vapor train as well as it pulled extra carriages than anybody had actually ever bothered to count. Running the length of the train was a passage which seemed lit by little gas lamps. The strange thing was that Nina had actually been to museums with gas lamps and there was something various about the lights on the train. As she leaned more detailed the flicker of the light inside looked less like a flame and even more like a.

firebug or - and she actually hoped this wasn't the situation - a little fairy trapped inside. As she gazed, she could not see any kind of sign there was an animal in there and also decided it must instead be some type of magic at the workplace. Checking the carriage, Nina could see that the passage she stood in was about large enough for two guys to easily go by each other. Most interesting of all was that instead of the areas having chairs for the guests to sit in, there were stalls. Miniature stores, actually. Each one loaded from flooring to ceiling with the stallholders' unusual collections of trinkets and also curios. As well as it was here, in this wonderful area, on a train riding via the snowy hills of who-knew-where that Nina was particular she would discover brand-new gifts for her pals. She simply hadn't relied on just how a lot option would make picking something so really difficult .

**Chapter 3**

# THE CLOCKWORK BAZAAR

Nina pressed past a male as high as he was vast, the long hair on his fur layer scrubing versus her face as she did. It smelled of damp dog as well as Nina recoiled as it combed against her. Fragile, ornate boxes loaded the area she discovered herself in. A small, wrinkled female was curled in.
what appeared to be a pet basket in the corner yet she welcomed Nina warmly. "Hello flower," she croaked. Her voice was scratchy as well as high however with a.
heat Nina wasn't anticipating. "Look around, select things up, if you've got any inquiries simply shout.".
" Thank you," Nina smiled back. The female squinted at her.
" I can't hear you petal, you'll need to scream," the female responded. "My hearing is not what it once was.".
" THANK YOU!" Nina shouted.
The big male in the entrance transformed and frowned at her as well as Nina can see his face for the first time. His birdlike, bloodshot eyes sat under bushy black eyebrows. His beard had a thin, white red stripe in it as well as he had waxed his moustache into elaborate curls that virtually touched his cheekbones. Nina grabbed among the boxes and found that it has to have been inlaid with some kind of magical stone. As she turned it over in her hands it showed up to change colour. There was a hold on the front and as Nina released it, the cover sprang open. The box began to play a tune a little like a songs box. However rather than the plink-plink you would anticipate to hear the audio was deeper, a lot more resonant as if there were miniature elves playing trumpets as well as tubas someplace within. She very carefully shut the lid as well as positioned it back on the rack.
Probably that would be the type of point that Ivy would certainly like. Nina.

reasoned, Ivy had lately ended up being a big sis. If Nina might get her something that would settle her infant bro to sleep after that her friend could invest more time playing video games as well as less time dropping off when she read books at institution.

" Thank you," Nina said to the old lady however she appeared to be asleep in her makeshift bed so Nina simply walked silently back out right into the corridor.

She wandered through the train, practically hypnotised by the fantastic little bits and bobs that bordered her in each new area she visited. There were clothes and fabric, sculptures of timber as well as rock, toys that danced on their own as well as individuals selling food over fires they had actually lit on the flooring. Nina discovered herself wondering exactly how the fires didn't melt an opening through the wooden floor of the carriage but when she asked among the stallholders he just grumbled at her so she made a sharp exit.

Out of the windows Nina could see a wintery landscape as the train sped its means forward. It appeared they were travelling via a land of snow drifts, white-topped hillsides as well as areas all deep with snow. The carriages were cozy, most likely due to all the people but each time she got to completion of a carriage the freezing cold would certainly bite at her even through her coat. Each carriage held 3 or 4 stalls and afterwards there was a hefty door. Nina soon understood that you can just unlock of the carriage and walk to the next one. Only it had not been quite that easy. When you opened the door you discovered on your own outside, the snow whipping around you and also the cold permeating to your bones.

The doors all opened up inwards due to the fact that there was so little room in between the carriages. The reason for this was easy; the only things that were outdoors were a ladder to provide the train's guards accessibility to the roof as well as the combinings listed below that held the carriages together. To get from one carriage to the following you had to jump from the small wood system on one side to the small wood system on the various other. Fall and also slip and also you would certainly more than likely find yourself plunging onto the track where the carriages behind would certainly rumbling over you, slicing you right into little portions no larger than apples as well as leaving you as dead as it's possible to be.

Needless to say Nina was very careful as she jumped from carriage to carriage. As well as dive she did, from the very first to the second, the 2nd to the third et cetera. One carriage each time she learnt a relatively limitless ceremony of people marketing whatever from items that did that- knows-what to pets she was particular didn't exist outside of storybooks.

Bearing in mind that she was in a storybook, Nina glanced at her watch and after that smiled to herself. It felt like she had gone to the Clockwork Bazaar for about a hr yet actually the time would certainly be passing a lot more slowly. She, Ivy and also Oswald had actually invested days, occasionally also longer, having adventures only to return and for it to be later on the same mid-day back in the Lost Bookshop.
As her buddies' names danced via her head she saw a store which resembled it might have just things Oswald would such as.

# Chapter 4

## THE HUNT FOR PRESENTS

"You like?" a high, spindly foreign gent that looked a little cross- looked at behind his jam-jar eyeglasses asked her.

The compartment teemed with all sort of binoculars and also telescopes, from amplifying glasses to opera glasses. Actually, anything that would make the more away appear better. Nina had spotted one set of binoculars that she believed might be ideal for Oswald. She transformed them over in her hands, they were covered with an exotic leather. She put them to her eyes and was startled to locate the whole of the train disappeared and she can see the constellations in the evening sky. Other than that it was still daytime.

" Wow, these are ..." she began.

" Very unique, no?" the male winked at her, his eyes looking massive, multiplied behind his glasses. "I give excellent trade. What you obtained?".

Nina was sure that Oswald would enjoy the binoculars. His Dad had actually acquired him a telescope for his birthday celebration earlier in the year as well as he had become stressed with stargazing ever since.

" Very special, yes," Nina nodded. Up up until this point she wasn't actually sure how she was going to trade with the stallholders. She had some spending money in a purse in her satchel yet she was persuaded that these magical storybook individuals wouldn't also know what genuine cash looked like. As well as from what the thin man was claiming, he really did not want money. He intended to exchange. "I'm unsure ...".

" I provide you this," he stated and propelled a book into her hand. Guide was called 'The Magic of the Night Sky: Seeing The Stars Between The Stars'. "Magic book, magic goggle." He responded enthusiastically at her.

" You go, trade," he claimed, observing that Nina was patting her pockets and also bag in a method that suggested she didn't have enough. "I maintain for you. You return, no?".

" No," claimed Nina. "I mean, yes. If I can get something you like.".

" I like all kind things," he smiled once again and ushered her out of his compartment. "Goodbye tiny girl.".

Back in the corridor Nina laughed at being called 'little woman'. She would need to locate something she might trade for. Maybe if she maintained trading she might locate a trinket he would such as. It couldn't be that difficult in a place similar to this, could it? Now all she had to do was discover an existing for Ivy.

The idea that she might obtain something for her best friend maintained going around her head as she one more time pushed past the guy with the pointy beard as well as moustache as well as the fuzzy layer. Like everyone else he appeared to be looking for a very certain point yet with so much on offer it was difficult to choose what to opt for. A number of jumps from carriage to carriage later on, nevertheless, and also Nina assumed she had actually lastly found the excellent present.

Presiding over the compartment-shop was a more youthful woman, around the very same age as Nina's Mum. She was worn what Nina envisioned an old-made gypsy could use, a floral outfit floating regarding her as she wafted occasionally around her store and a lace stole curtained over her shoulder. Her long, black hair seemed so dark it was like the evening skies in winter season.

" I bring you songs," was all she stated as she gestured in the direction of the oddest collection of musical instruments Nina had ever before seen.

Some she assumed she may know the names of, a bongo right here, a banjo there however others were such odd as well as remarkable forms, with several strings and nozzles for blowing in she had no idea what they were.

" Is that a ukulele?" she asked, indicating a tool that looked for all the world like a shrunken guitar but with 4 strings as opposed to six.

The lady blinked her lengthy eyelashes and smiled. "I see we have a specialist in the shop.".

Nina blushed a little. "Er, n-no," she stammered. "I do not recognize what a great deal of these are, I just like that one. It's an existing for my buddy.".

The woman picked as well as nodded up the ukulele. The deep, deep purple of its body radiated brilliantly versus the white of the snow rushing past on the embankments outside the window. The lady lifted the ukulele as well as played three crystal-clear notes upon it.

Nina instantly felt her eyelids getting heavy and also her head responded forward but the woman quit playing and clapped her hands noisally. Nina's eyes snapped open and also she stared at the woman.

" Is it ..." Nina stopped briefly, uncertain of the word she was searching for. "Enchanted?".

The female chuckled a transmittable laugh as well as touched Nina's shoulder. "Yes," she stated. "Of course it is. Whatever I sell is ensured, one hundred percent captivated.".

" Good to recognize," claimed Nina with a laugh. "I was looking for something for my buddy. She has an infant brother. He's new and he doesn't rest.".

The girl brushed the neck of the ukulele as well as responded. "This will certainly be excellent for her. A few notes before bedtime as well as ..." she shut her eyes and placed her head to one side.

Nina smiled. "I'll take it," she claimed. "Excellent. So what do you need to trade?".

Nina iced up. What did she need to trade? What did she have that the woman would certainly absorb exchange for the wonderful tool? She stood up her index finger. "One moment," she claimed.

Opening her bag, Nina searched around inside. Fifty percent a packet of mints? No. An utilized cells? Eew, no. A comic? Probably not. And after that she noticed that around her wrist was her watch. A digital watch. They likely really did not have watches in the Clockwork Bazaar, she assumed. As a matter of fact, the name was a telltale sign - 'clockwork'. She slid the watch off as well as revealed it to the girl with the ukulele.

The girl stared at the numbers on the face for a few secs and after that stated, rather merely, "No.".

# Chapter 5

# NINA'S MULTI-SHOP SWAP

What do you mean 'no'?" asked Nina, forgetting her manners for a moment. Capturing herself she proceeded, "It's simply that I do not.
have anything else to trade, what should I do?".
The lady took the ukulele as well as placed it hidden under among the makeshift counters on which her enchanting music tools were set down.
" I'll keep it to one side for you," stated the girl with a smile. "If you can discover something I such as then it's yours. Does that audio reasonable?".
Nina nodded. "So I should trade my watch with a person who desires it for something you want and then I can obtain the ukulele?".
The girl nodded. There was a noise in the shop behind Nina and also the lady dipped into her shoulder to welcome an additional client.
" Just another thing," said Nina. "What sort of things do you like?" "Well, visitors like me like nothing greater than leaving under the.
stars ...".
Nina gasped. "I think I saw something you 'd such as! I'll be back really soon." She spun around and also evaded right into the corridor, pressing past the huge, pointy-bearded guy. , if she really did not recognize far better she would virtually be convinced he was following her.
.

Galloping past stall after delay, squeezing through crowds of individuals, hopping from carriage to carriage, Nina made her way as quick as she might back to the tall, spindly store owner with the jam-jar spectacles.
" Small lady!" he tossed his arms out and also his eyes widened. Exaggerated by his spectacles there was nothing but 2 massive white circles with small black places in the middle. "You back for my fine spyglasses?".
" I really hope so," Nina gave the man what she hoped was a winning smile. "Werry vell," he stated. "Show me what you are having.".

Nina took the digital watch from her bag, holding it reverently as if it were an item of unmatched worth as well as charm.

The slim man put his lips with each other and also made a lengthy piercing raspberry sound.

" Is votch?" he asked. "Votch?" asked Nina. "Votch. Inform time. Votch." "Oh, yes. Votch. Watch." "Like I state ... votch.".

" Do you like it?" asked Nina.

" No," he stated. "But I maintain publication as well as spyglasses for you. You go profession for something little and quite. Not ticky or tocky.".

When she got here, and also at once Nina recognized what she needed to do and also bounded off to the initial delay she would certainly seen. If she would trade, she picked up the quite little songs box and asked the old lady in a loud as well as clear voice.

The old woman groaned in reply and motioned Nina to reveal her what she had to trade. Nina meticulously obtained the digital watch and also revealed the old woman.

" Perfect!" the lady said. "Perfect?" asked Nina. "Except it's no great, petal.".

" What?" Nina blurted out. How much time could this take place? Would she need to trade as well as trade and also trade throughout the day up until she found somebody - anybody - who would switch with her? "You stated it was perfect.".

" Mmmm," said the old woman as well as smacked her wrinkly lips with each other. "I did. And also it would certainly be. Yet if it obtains a little dark then I won't have the ability to see it. My eyes aren't what they used to be.".

Nina sighed and was about to transform and leave when she remembered something. She pushed among the switches on the side of the display and also the watch illuminated. The old lady almost fell out of her basket.

" My, my. Will wonders never cease?" the old lady smiled a smile that was more periodontal than teeth. "You've obtained a deal, petal.".

And before Nina actually knew what was occurring the watch had vanished from her hands and been replaced by the stunning music box. Nina blinked, breathed and after that ran down the train once more.

" Is a bargain!" the high man with the jam-jar eyeglasses said practically before Nina had actually even taken the music box out of her bag. His spindly fingers appeared to crawl via the air, plucking package from her and opening the cover. As quickly as the songs came, the man's eyes closed as well as he started to delicately waltz around the tiny compartment. "Such charm. Please to take the spyglasses. And not forget the book. Exists. Free to you.".

Nina thanked the shopkeeper and slid guide right into her bag prior to hanging the field glasses around her neck. She adjusted them to ensure they wouldn't hinder then dashed off down the corridor.

Nina wasn't quite ready for what she located when she returned to the gypsy-lady's area.

**Chapter 6**

# IS THIS A SLEEPER CARRIAGE?

She realised that something had not been fairly appropriate the minute she leapt the void and unlocked to the carriage. It was quiet.

Well, not totally silent. Of course, the noise of the train was still clackety-clacking in the background but there was nothing else. As quickly as the carriage door broke closed behind her, Nina froze.

On the flooring in front of her was a teenage girl. Behind the woman was a slightly older young boy. In the doorway of the first area was an Irish wolfhound, a dog so big that Nina would barely have actually been able to see over its back if it had been standing.

But it had not been. As well as neither was the girl and also neither was the child. In fact, everybody Nina could see was on the flooring. Fearing the most awful, she went down to her knees and reached out, taking the wrist of the girl dropped directly before her as well as checking for a pulse. She couldn't locate one and her heart began to race in panic yet then she remembered something that Oswald stated his big sibling had actually done to him ...

Nina moved to the woman's head. Her eyes and mouth were closed and her black hair had actually fallen across her face. She reached out her finger and thumb and pinched the woman's nose. Even unconscious, the lady intuitively opened her mouth as well as started breathing in this way rather.

When she squeezed their noses, Nina took a breath a sigh of relief as the first couple of people she tipped over all opened their mouths. Carefully making her way via the carriage, she inspected all the shopkeepers and the consumers. If the substantial pet was still alive, there was no requirement to check. She might tell it was having a great dream due to the fact that its front and back legs kept jerking and also it's long tail sometimes wagged as well as knocked ornaments off a shelf alongside it.

By the time Nina got to the gypsy lady she had all but forgotten the factor she had returned. Concerning the ukulele. The gypsy woman lay on the flooring of her area, her legs tangled and also her head lolling forward so her chin touched her chest. Nina clambered nimbly around behind the counter. She carefully raised the lady's head, relaxing it delicately against the wall behind her. She was about to hold her nose when her eyes flickered and she groaned.

" Are you all right?" asked Nina silently so as not to surprise the girl.

"Mnuuuuurm," the woman groaned in action. Nina browsed and also. identified a high, glass container full of clear fluid. Recognizing that things weren't constantly what they seemed in position like The Clockwork Bazaar, Nina uncorked the bottle and provided it a lengthy smell. It really did not scent of anything so she took the tiniest of small sips. Tasted regular. It really did not feel like it was a cure-all or anything like that. She made a decision there was a likelihood it was water.

" Here, take a sip," claimed Nina, holding the container approximately the lady's lips.

The gypsy girl handled to take a little sip, her tired mouth letting a few of the water drop onto her outfit. As soon as extra, her tongue touched her lips a couple of times after that her eyes trembled. Nina waited patiently, looking for a sign that the girl wanted a lot more water yet she appeared to be focusing on another thing. A few moments later, and with a massive amount of effort, she took care of to open both eyes simply a fracture.

" Thief," the slurred word appeared of the gypsy girl's mouth.

The bottom fell out of Nina's stomach at the idea of being called a thief as well as she began to stammer the lady however a reply disturbed.

" Thief took it. Sorry.".

Nina gave the lady and responded's arm a little press of confidence. "I'll aid you, don't stress," she claimed.

It didn't take long, maybe 2 or 3 mins for the girl to open her eyes right as well as start to talk without slurring her words. She seemed incapable to rise as well as, evaluating by the moans and chatter that were starting to re-enter the carriage, some of the other inhabitants were waking up also.

" Why are you sorry?" Nina asked, giving the gypsy woman a couple of even more sips of water.

Before the woman can speak points started to add up in Nina's head. The fatigue, a thief ... someone had stolen the ukulele and used it to cover their tracks by sending everyone in the carriage to rest. And afterwards she noticed another thing. People were awakening in a type of order. The people.

closest to the gypsy lady's shop compartment were beginning to mix first with individuals down the other end of the cabin still asleep. If she was creative she could utilize this to track the thief.
" I'm pursuing him," said Nina. She stood as well as took the binoculars from around her neck. "I got these for you ... You recognize ... to trade.".
The gypsy lady shook her head. "Let it go, little woman. He was a big guy, he'll only subdue you.".
This was like a red flag to a bull to Nina. She despised being called 'little woman'. What was so bad concerning not being a grown up? However worse still, she disliked that people may believe that since she was a girl, she could not do something. She carefully positioned the binoculars on the gypsy's counter and gave her a pleasant smile. "You do not need to be big to get the better of a person. You just need to be creative," Nina claimed.
The gypsy female provided an amazed smile. "You will certainly succeed in life, I assume.".
" What did he look like?" asked Nina. "If you can bear in mind.".
The gypsy lady nodded. "He was a huge man, as tall as the carriage roof covering almost. And large also, he loaded the entrance of my shop. He had a beard with a white streak down the center ...".
" A moustache that was twirled right into points and a long, hairy coat?" Nina disrupted.
The gypsy lady looked a little taken aback. "How did you recognize?" Nina shrugged. "I see points.".
And also with that, she took off.

**Chapter 7**

# IN THE SNOW AND ON THE ROOF

Spublishing toward the sleepiest end of the carriage, Nina tossed unlock. The snow whipped in, the cool instantly biting at her skin. She attempted to ignore it, stepping out anyhow. She jumped the gap where the carriages were paired with each other as well as unlocked to the next carriage. Entering its welcoming cozy glow she was greeted with a comparable scene to the one she had found in the previous carriage. The young, old, tall, brief,.
slim and also fat, all lying awkwardly on the ground fast asleep.
Nina swiftly picked her means via them, assuming all the time, trying to come up with a strategy. What did she know? She recognized that he was large and also big and also as a result would not have the ability to pick his method through the sleeping people as quickly as her. She recognized that it would take a little time to send out the people to sleep. He would certainly have to play as well as stand, making sure everyone was asleep before going on. And that offered her a benefit. It suggested that she can catch up with him. Afterwards? Well she had not been certain however she would consider something.
She bounded onward, relocating rapidly from the warmth of the carriage to the biting cold of the outdoors and also back into the heat of the following carriage. It coincided tale there, the sleepers rested much deeper and there were even more of them yet otherwise it was identical. And also the exact same for the next carriage. And the following.
Nina wondered how much time this might go on, she knew the train was unbelievably long, magically long you could say yet at some point they had to get to the front. And then she tipped from the cold of the outside into the warmth of a carriage and also every little thing was various. No-one was asleep. No- one was getting up. No-one was panicked. And there was no indicator of the burglar. She made a quick assessment of the carriage, asked among the storekeepers if.

they had seen the thief but they hadn't. And then a thought occurred to her.

She fastened her coat tight and stepped outside to the area between the carriages. Sure enough; next to the ladder that led to the train's roof, snagged on a piece of rough wood, was a clump of long hair. The exact colour and length of the hair on the thief's coat.

Taking a deep breath, Nina gripped the first rung of the metal ladder. It was freezing against her fingers and for a moment she thought about just letting him go but if there was one thing she couldn't resist it was the thrill of adventure. Plus she couldn't very well let her best friend Ivy go without a present at Christmas, could she?

The cold penetrated her fingers all the way to the bone as she climbed. One hand over the other, from rung to rung until she reached the roof of the train. She squinted as she poked her head up, the snow somehow managing to drive itself through her eyelashes and make her eyeballs cold. She turned to look towards the back of the train, it seemed to stretch off forever into the blizzard but there was no sign of the pointy-bearded thief. Screwing up her eyes as closed as she could without actually closing them, Nina turned to face the front of the train and that was when she saw him.

Although there were perhaps only a half a dozen carriages between them, his outline seemed faint and distant. She wondered for a second if it was the thief but the size of him and the long-haired coat were unmistakable. Nina hoisted herself the rest of the way onto the roof of the train and took her first step forward. Now I don't know if you've ever climbed onto the top of a moving train before. I expect you probably haven't. If you have I would advise you not to tell your Mum or Dad. Parents tend to frown on things like that. But if you *had* climbed on top of a moving train one of the first things you would notice would be how fast the ground moves beneath you. Well, that and just how splattered you would be if you hit it. There are no handrails or barriers to stop you falling off save a tiny, raised lip on the very edge. Go past that, you fall off the top of the train and it's game over for you.

Or in this case, for Nina. She stepped forward, carefully planting one boot down in the light dusting of snow before striding the next forward. At the end of the carriage Nina climbed down the ladder, jumped across the short gap to the next carriage, then clambered up the ladder and on to the roof of the next. Except the thief was getting away. He was jumping from one carriage to the next instead of climbing down and Nina knew that she would have to do the same if she was going to catch him.

To be sure she would make the jump, Nina knew that she would have to take a run up and so instead of the sure, steady steps, she sprinted. From the back of the carriage she had climbed she ran as fast as her legs would carry her and was about to reach the edge and jump when…

She skidded to a halt. Her nerve had gone. The train was going so fast and the gap seemed so much bigger up here. And then, in a moment, the snow stopped. The storm seemed to evaporate and the winter sun lit up the roof of the train all the way to the locomotive puffing steam into the air.

Nina blinked the last of the snow from her eyes, jogged to the back of the carriage again, took a deep breath and ran. Step after step she sprinted, her breath quickening until it felt like she was breathing with the same *clackety-clack* rhythm as the train on the tracks and she jumped. High into the air, arms windmilling as she went over the gap between the two carriages.

She landed heavily on the next carriage and was about to allow herself a grin when, instead of slowing down as she thought she would, she slid. The snow underfoot hid ice and her feet just… *kept going*. She tumbled onto her bum, putting her hands out to stop herself but still she slid. Although she was slowing down a little, first one foot, then the other went over the edge until-

*Thunk*

She hit the rail at the edge and gripped it tightly. At last, she stopped sliding.

But the noise and the bright sunlight had caught the attention of the man she was chasing.

He stared at her as she got up. Stared at her as she dusted herself off, as she straightened her bag and got a steady footing. He even stared, unblinking as she ran the length of the carriage, jumping into the air and landing on the next carriage.

He was more than a little surprised to see that this time, instead of sliding or falling, Nina put her legs into the snow as if she was wearing ice skates and skidded half the length of the carriage before starting to sprint once more.

When she hit the edge of the next carriage and jumped again, even Nina could see the shock on his face. The sight of this girl hopping from carriage to carriage as if it was the most natural thing in the world caused his mouth to droop open in surprise. But his shock didn't last long and he began trying to throw things at her.

First snowballs. But she just ducked, ran, jumped and slid.

Then coins from his pockets. But she just ducked, ran, jumped and slid.

Then fruit from his bag. But she just ducked, ran, jumped and slid.

Finally, when Nina was just one carriage away and with a look of panic on his face he hurled something big. Something Nina wasn't sure what it was but she didn't want it to hit her so this time when she landed on the carriage she turned slightly and skidded to a halt. And the object, whatever it was, landed neatly at her feet.

Nina knelt down and picked up a crossbow with a strange sort of anchor on the end. A grappling iron. That might come in useful, she thought, and slipped it into her bag. Glancing up at the thief she rummaged in her bag once more, pulling out her earmuffs and putting them over her freezing ears before taking a run up and hurling herself through the air and sliding to a halt at the thief's feet.

"What on earth do you think you're doing little girl?" he sneered.

Nina was about to hop to her feet when he took out the ukulele and placed his fingers on the strings to play.

# Chapter 8

## OUTSMARTED BY A LITTLE GIRL?

L ittle girl.
      Why was it always 'little girl'?

Nina felt the cold, wet of the snow seeping through her jeans and the hot flush of anger in her cheeks. She knew what was about to happen. He was going to play the ukulele, she was going to fall asleep then the train would probably turn a sharp corner and she would slide off the roof and...

The thief began to strum the ukulele. He couldn't really play, Nina remembered thinking just before her eyes closed. Not half as well as Ivy could. She would *definitely* prefer listening to Ivy instead of him.

The music stopped and the thief gave Nina a nudge with his foot. She didn't move. He nodded to himself and looked up into the blue sky. One of the clouds up ahead looked darker than the others. He squinted, then smiled a smile of broken yellow teeth and pulled a small, square contraption from his pocket. Pressing a button on the side, he held it to his mouth and spoke with a thick French accent.

"I am in position. Are you ready to rendezvous? Over."

There was a crackle of static then another voice replied. "Do you have the item? Over."

The strange looking cloud was quickly getting bigger. It moved silently towards them as the train thundered forward down the track. If anyone apart from the thief had been awake on the roof, they would have seen that the cloud was not, in fact, a cloud but was some sort of Zeppelin.

"Oui. Yes. I have it. Over," said the thief as he took a couple of steps away from Nina. As he spoke, the sun caught the side of the airship and the silver gondola that hung at the bottom, holding the pilot and passengers.

"And the little girl?" asked the radio.

The man took a deep breath, clearly irritated by the question.

The Zeppelin turned so its side was facing the oncoming train. Had anyone else been on top of the train squinting through half-closed eyes, they might have spotted a rope ladder unfurling from the gondola.

"I don't know what the fuss was all about or why no one else has dealt with the little brat yet. It was a piece of cake."

"I am NOT a LITTLE GIRL!"

The thief spun around to see Nina, perfectly awake and standing right there on the roof of the carriage with no ill effects whatsoever.

"What?" asked the radio.

The thief glanced at the radio then back at Nina who was holding the grappling crossbow in a very threatening manner.

"Now, wait a minute," the thief put his hands up in pretend-surrender. He took a half a step away from her and his foot slipped ever-so slightly on the icy roof. "Let's talk about this, shall we?"

"Let's not," said Nina, who was cold from lying in the snow pretending to be asleep and angry at being patronised by idiotic adults. She pulled the trigger on the crossbow and the hook went flying over the thief's shoulder.

For a second he smiled, thinking she had missed and then his face dropped as he realised what she had done. He turned on the spot just in time to see the sharp hook punch a hole in the side of the Zeppelin.

"Mayday! Mayday!" the radio crackled.

The thief looked bewildered. How had this happened, what exactly was happening? He turned back to Nina as the Zeppelin began to sink out of the sky and towards the ground.

"You!"

Nina nodded. "Me," she said and reached out her left hand, snatching the ukulele from him.

"It won't work," he grinned his broken-toothed grin once more. "I see now you had those ear-covers. I have fingers!" And he shoved one dirty digit in each of his ears.

Nina bunched up her hand, pulled it back and punched him square in the nose.

Perhaps it was the sound of the Zeppelin crashing into the ground, perhaps it was the movement of the train, perhaps the ice underfoot, perhaps that he just didn't believe it would have any effect… whatever the reason, the punch did exactly what it was supposed to do and sent him down like a   sack of potatoes. As he landed, there was a cracking noise and then, with a puff of snow, the skylight he had fallen onto collapsed and he dropped into the carriage below.

Nina moved carefully forward, cautious in case another part of the roof might collapse too but, thankfully, it didn't. She looked into the dimly lit carriage below and was happy to see one of the train's guards standing over the unconscious body of the thief.

The train's guard peered up at her, a look of utter confusion on his face. Nina thought for a moment, the wind rushing through her hair, the roar of air and steam around her. She knew she couldn't explain properly from up on the roof. Or maybe at all.

"No ticket!" she shouted at the top of her voice then turned and carefully picked her way to the edge of the carriage. She climbed gingerly down the ladder. She was about to go and explain to the guard for real when, for some reason, she looked over her shoulder to the carriage behind. To her surprise, through the tiny, steamy window, she could have sworn that she saw the familiar outline of her Uncle Bill.

Stepping deftly over the gap, she threw open the carriage door and stepped inside but instead of the carriage she expected it was pitch black. She spun around but the door snapped shut behind her and when she stumbled forward she couldn't find the handle any more. Out of nowhere the noise from the train began to get louder. The snow from outside burst in from somewhere and began swirling around her. Faster and faster it span, getting thicker and thicker until, with a thunderous bang, everything stopped and everything went dark.

**Chapter 9**

# CHRISTMAS IN THE LOST BOOKSHOP

When she opened her eyes Nina was sitting on the familiar wooden floor of the hidden room in the Lost Bookshop. Her hand throbbed from when she'd hit the thief, her teeth chattered with the cold but she was back in the bookshop once more.

She took a deep breath; the smell of the books filled her nose. She blinked away the snow… or was it dust? Standing up she took off the earmuffs and coat and put them on a nearby chair. Without her watch she had no idea how long she had been away from her friends. And what she was going to do about Oswald's present? In spite of all her best efforts, she'd returned to the Lost Bookshop before she could trade anything for him.

Locking the door of the hidden room as quietly as she could, Nina's shoulders sagged. One present. And it wasn't even wrapped.

"I thought I better check you hadn't been crushed under a pile of falling books," Nina's Uncle Bill appeared from somewhere with a smile but his smile turned to concern when he saw Nina's face. "Everything alright?"

Nina shrugged. "I hurt my hand getting Ivy's present," she said. "And Oswald's was ruined because the rain got into the shop window."

Uncle Bill stroked his grey beard and raised an eyebrow at her.

"What?" she asked.

Uncle Bill pointed at Nina's bag. "What's that sticking out of your bag?"

Nina looked down at her satchel and, sure enough, a book poked out. The book on magical astronomy she had been given with the binoculars. In all the excitement she had completely forgotten about it. Oswald was the biggest bookworm Nina had ever met. If anything he'd probably like the book more than anything else she could think to give him!

"Oh yes!" Nina grinned. "I completely forgot about that."

"Now run along, your friends have been waiting patiently for the last ten minutes," said Uncle Bill, giving Nina a hug. "I'll ask you Aunty Ann for some ice for that hand."

"What's the matter with her hand?" Aunty Ann's voice floated in from a nearby room. "Did you punch your Uncle Bill on the conk for not selling any books? I know I sometimes feel like it."

"Something like that!" Nina shouted back before running along to go and swap presents with her friends.

"I think your hot chocolate might've got cold," said Ivy. "You were gone a while."

Nina held the ukulele behind her back so that Ivy couldn't see. "I know," she said. "I had a little trouble getting your presents."

"Hang on a minute," said Oswald, a frown knitting itself across his brow. "What took you so long?"

"Long story," said Nina, giving her friends a wink. "I got these for you. Sorry they're not wrapped. There was… a problem."

Nina took the book from her bag and the ukulele from behind her back and held them out for her friends.

"The Magic of the Night Sky : Seeing The Stars Between The Stars," Oswald read from the cover. "This is so cool. Is it…"

Nina coughed to stop Oswald saying the words. He got the message and took to excitedly flipping through the pages.

Ivy was about to strum the ukulele but Nina put her hand over the strings. "Maybe wait a little while before you do that," she said. "I need to explain how it works…"

"But I know…" Ivy began.

Nina coughed again. "I'll explain before you do. It's different. Special. Might help your little brother get to sleep," Nina said. Ivy's eyes widened as she realised what her friend was saying. "Might help anyone get to sleep if you're not careful…" Nina added under her breath.

"Your turn!" Ivy and Oswald chorused, both of them grabbing the presents they had bought for Nina and shoving them into her arms.

As Nina warmed herself by the fire opening her presents with her friends, she smiled. She was so happy her friends loved their presents and she couldn't wait for the new year when they could come back to the Lost Bookshop and have another adventure. No-one else knew about their secret, that hidden room that led to adventures, no-one in the world.

But the children knew. And I know. And you know.
And Aunty Ann and Uncle Bill?
Well, you never know what they know.